*To every thing there is a season,
and a time to every purpose under heaven.*

— ECCLESIASTES 3:1

HEAVEN

PHOTOGRAPHS BY TERRY DONNELLY
TEXT BY ROBIN MAGOWAN

ON EARTH

A miniSeries book
ABBEVILLE PRESS PUBLISHERS
NEW YORK   LONDON

CONTENTS

The combined essences of heaven
and earth became the yin and yang,
the concentrated essences
of the yin and yang became
the four seasons, and the
scattered essences of the four seasons
became the myriad creatures
of the world.

—HUAI-NAN TZU

THE SEASONS

In speaking of the seasons we usually mean spring, summer, fall, and winter. But why confine ourselves to four? Aren't there any number of seasons overlapping and recurring within any one season? Or are four too many? New Englanders would argue there are only two—winter and the Fourth of July. Californians might agree, only their year falls in the African manner into a season of winter wet, followed (in non-El Niño years) by eight months of dryness and increasing heat. The European concept of four more or less equal seasons is not one that fits our various realities very accurately. But is that reason enough to junk it and all its associations?

The deeper our sense of nature, the more sharply we are likely to feel the differences brought into being by the earth's somewhat wobbling rotation about its solar axis: the angles of the light; the play of the winds; the mysterious recurrences of birds and flowers; the speed of the changes, week by week, in a garden, a mountain side, or even along a cycling path. This seasonal time gives us a way of addressing our own human time. It's hard to see change in one's self. But we can spot changes in the seasonal mirror that can teach us how to attune ourselves to our own changing moments.

In a big city a seasonal awareness is not easily come by. But anyone working outdoors or living in the country can't help but be affected by the seasonal changes. Yet few, probably, are as influenced as the farmer. For a farmer, almost each day carries a distinctive message, when to plant this or harvest that. I once knew a man who went to agricultural school and did everything he could to turn himself into a farmer. But, not growing up in a farming home, he didn't possess that built-in calendar, and thus he failed.

As a people the Japanese are very highly attuned to seasonal differences. An ikebana flower arranger is doing more than making a pleasing bouquet out of the shapes and smells and colors that a moment offers. Instead, he is trying in his arrangement to capture the very look, say, of March itself—the threat and uncertainty in the air, the quickness of the light, the way the wind hurls everything about.

The Japanese break up the year into a sequence of

flower festivals, from the first camellias all the way to the last chrysanthemums. Each has its rites, its special shrine where people go to peer, to sniff, to make themselves more Japanese. On a drizzly, bone-cold March evening it's instructive to come upon a million worshipers huddled beneath the spotlit cherry trees in Tokyo's Ueno Park. Not all, of course, are gazing at the pink and white buds. Their ancestors, they explain, have more than taken care of that. Instead they are drinking, raising cups to this three-week spectacle of beauty and evanescence—the buds and the drifting petals—that surrounds them. As Buddhists, they realize the world they inhabit is a world of dew. But that makes celebrating their own momentariness all the more crucial.

For those of us raised in the Judeo-Christian tradition nature is an obstacle to be triumphed over. The Christian year in which everything is packed into those four winter months (birth near the shortest day, death in early spring) teaches us how to do just that and attain everlasting life. The remainder of the year, sowing the fields, bringing in the crops, may not quite be relaxation. But it's what people living on the land have traditionally done to survive. Between the winter of prayer and the summer of husbandry there appears to have been an acceptable balance.

Spring

For us New Year's Day—"the birth of hope," Thomas Jefferson called it—falls in the dead of winter, exactly between Christmas and Epiphany. More in tune with nature are those whose year begins with the vernal equinox. For the Persians this "Norus" or New Year is a ten-day celebration, time enough for a family to return to their native village and give each other the new clothes the occasion requires.

Where I live in New England, that might be less acceptable. March has a bad repute. It ushers in the season of mud that lasts well into April. Anyone who can hastens to get away. But if there is not as yet much to feast your eyes on, there is more than enough to listen to, from the soughing of the wind to the various songs of the birds, each male taunting his fellows with his particular take on, "All day, all night, with Mary Ann." Over and over, can one ever have too much of a good song?

If it gets a little deafening, then head out to the deep forest. There may not be much in the way of greenery, but everywhere you stroll there is the sound and visual joy of cascading water. That sound of winter melting away is a profoundly spiritual one. It is as if the earth itself were waking up from its winter nap.

The goal of a spiritual life is often said to be the attainment of a state of enlightenment. But enlightenment, hard won as it may be, is a relatively passive state, requiring nothing from us. Better, the Buddha thought, to live each moment fully awake. It's that first awakening he experienced sitting under a bodhi tree outside Benares.

When we come upon nature's equivalent of that awakening, it is usually against a foggy overcast, a sign of the battle between warm air and cold earth. Picture beneath the fog snow, perhaps some black rocks outlining a frozen stream. Descend a ways and there, black as life, will be a first gush of water. That joyful outpouring sets in motion the musical overture of the forthcoming year.

Summer

If spring is the time of awakening, of arrival, of those three-hour long twilit cloud shows and soft magical dusks, then summer is the time of bounty. It is not one set of bulbs that is arriving—snow drops one week, crocuses the next—but everything seems to be popping up all at once, one garden or meadow layer higher than the next. To our surprise, our astonishment, day by day it all keeps turning into something else, eggs into fledglings, tadpoles into frogs, plants into stalks and stalks into flowers. It is this seasonal spectacle of growth, of transformation, that kindles something in us. The need to get out, to travel, to discover possibilities that, in making us more responsive, more open, will also transform us.

Where to go? One can do a lot worse than head out to the spectacular canyon lands and glacier-white mountain ranges of the Far West. From the moss-dripping trees of the Olympic rain forest to Mount Rainier and the Cascades, to the Grand Tetons and virtually anywhere in the great shimmering length of the Rockies, to the upland beauty of the inter-mountain high desert and Montana's Big Sky country, wherever you go the land offers an unparalleled grandeur. In the dry air you shake off the mugginess, the lassitude, the swamp bugs of the East and South, and you feel yourself stepping with an unexpected vigor. If "awe," as Joseph Campbell rightly claims, "is what moves us forward," then don a pair of walking shoes, or better yet riding boots, or even a wide-tired mountain bike, and set out: meadows flowering high as your chest; brilliantly colored tiny alpines blossoming in the tundra above a treeline; unpeopled ponds where you can pitch a tent and perhaps make a breakfast of a trout, a pike, you have just hooked.

If water lures you, then rent a canoe, or go down the Snake, the Green, the Colorado on a white water rafting trip, taking time to swim, to fish, to look up at the mountain eminences towering above. Many of them you can climb, passing through successive North American time zones as you mount, everything from Canadian boreal forest to arctic tundra.

This western change of scene, with all its newness, its restorative wonder—and "wonder is," as the Greeks knew, "the beginning of wisdom"—can't help but bring a perspective to the life you have left. When you return home you may look the same, but something decisive has happened. You are running now, not to someone else's but to your own internal clock.

Fall

We all have a favorite season, and mine is fall, because of the beauty of the light. Light is not something we are much conscious of when we are young. But the older we get, the more the light speaks until it seems synonymous with all that we bring to it. In opening to the light, we are opening to the fugitive moment we inhabit. It is the same readiness, this quickness of response, that fall encourages us to live by. We may not be able to accomplish all we once did. But that need not keep us from becoming, as we stand by a fence, or walk under the leaves, vibrant pieces of light ourselves.

In the summer the light, falling vertically, does not single things out. We see a tree trunk, not the light that sets the colors of the bark and its mottling of lichen aglow. In fall the light, pouring from a sun set lower on the horizon, strikes on an angle and, in striking, reveals. For the first time we are aware of the aliveness, the vibrancy, that whole other visual reality which shadows confer.

The "lustre" that Shelley speaks of in the autumn sky is not without a tinge of mourning—for the glory we have witnessed. But would that we too could leave the earth in a like orchestral blaze—all those different reds, golds, oranges, pinks. Whereas October brings the enormous surprise of the harvest moon, a great pumpkin all aglow just over that near hill. For a few weeks we sense how achingly beautiful and mysterious the earth is.

Winter

For the poet Mallarmé winter is "the creative season," when the mind at last comes into its own. The dense fabric of green that has been enclosing us has now vanished, as if stripped away. In its place there stands forth, newly revealed, an underlying bonework of rocks, distant hillsides, conifers, and frozen brooks. For some who inhabit an all too short-lit world of overcast skies and dominant lakes, winter can present a rather black prospect. But all nature need do is add a little snow—the merest inch or two—and all those dead deciduous forests return to instant radiance.

Where earth is hard, snow is soft, watery and, like the mind, reflective. Only it is the light that the snow picks up and reflects, a low, densely saturated light that keeps changing color from one moment to the next as it plumbs the prism of the snow. And the long, long shadows the trees cast are not black any longer, but a pale blue, a pale aspen gold. Among these stark sensuous contrasts of white and black our eyes float until we seem to be almost pieces of shadowed blue ourselves. What we all want, Henri Michaux remarks in Ecuador, is to have a body the color of the sky. And it's that very body winter gives us.

It's not all that hard to get out in it. When a river first freezes over, we can skate upstream on black ice, clambering around the little waterfalls to penetrate a forest otherwise unknown. When snow makes such forays impossible, we can strap on skis, or a pair of snowshoes, and pole off, enjoying the wind-proof enclosure of a forest, the visual exhilaration of an open field above a lake, with mountains tailing off blue in the background. Three or four days of below freezing nights and a cloud of silver dew, or hoarfrost, will start billowing forth from under the boughs of the pines and forest cedars. It's enough to turn us all into photographers, as we try to capture the blues and silvers of the spooky, billowing vapor. Then in the clear, star-heavy nights we may encounter the spectral green flash of aurora borealis, the northern lights. It may be only in winter that a landscape leaves behind its human imprint and comes into its own as a world apart.

It is this beautiful, yet forbidding world winter brings us. No wonder that creative sparks are set loose, shivering, from us.

HALF TITLE PAGE:

Fall view of Mount Shuksan and reflection on Picture Lake.
Mount Baker-Snoqualmie National Forest, Washington

TITLE PAGE:

Pfeiffer Beach seastacks silhouetted in sunset's afterglow.
Los Padres National Forest, California

SPRING

SPRING

We each have our ways of observing and celebrating the reawakening of the earth. That's why we turn out in droves for baseball's Opening Day, or join our angler companions for the opening of the fishing season. Or we go to the woods, the mountains, seeking out in our impatience the first false hellebores, the snowdrops and crocuses, and the other snow-melt mountain apparitions.

For me, the great spectacle of spring comes with the return of the forest birds. We have, to be sure, our winter residents. But they mostly come in earth grays and browns, whereas the warblers returning from the tropic winter are appareled in colors that seem to be joy itself. And, unlike the corresponding fall revisitation, the spring birds, even those who frequent the canopy, stand out

PREVIOUS PAGE:
Eagle Creek's Punchbowl Falls,
set in a moss- and fern-covered basalt gorge.
Mount Hood National Forest, Columbia Gorge National Scenic Area, Oregon

against the bright, thinly leafed greens. But it is the numbers, the sheer volume of activity, at your head and every other level, all of it working its way north as it feeds, that makes the spectacle. To catch it you don't have to go to one of the renowned staging areas, such as the Texas Gulf Coast or eastern Michigan's Point Pelee. Almost any city park can, on a given day, yield a like miracle.

If you are not looking up at the birds in the woods, you can be looking down at the virtual carpet of spring beauties flowering at your feet. Because plants expend so much of their vital energy flowering, they prefer to do it when the woods are still wet and cool enough. Whereas in the meadows and gardens the flowers can arrive in successive stages, each layer blossoming taller than the last. By mid-May the daffodils are up as are most of the tulips. While not much is blooming in the perennial beds, the alpine flowers of the rock garden are making the most of the last of the spring melt. Tiny cushion-like plants, but with comparatively large and striking flowers, catch them wavering in the wind of a mountainside, beckoning in all their variety, to the scant bees. The trees, in turn, provide a separate calendar of their own, beginning with the winter-blooming leatherwood and witch-hazel, and progress-

ing by way of forsythia, hawthorn, magnolia, and lilac to the last oaks. In spring, each flower, each tree, each bird, seems for a brief time its own miracle.

It is not only the birds and the bees who experience a quickening of the blood. The spring awakening is ours as well. Some of us, regularly as clockwork, find ourselves newly in love every April. This spring fever can, of course, get out of hand. That's why so many colleges now end their year in that month. Wiser perhaps our medieval ancestors who were encouraged to ride out to the woods, once a year, on May Day, with the lady of their choice. This day of license gave birth to a variety of songs, or reveries, toasting the greening of the year; the ritual source, we were once told, of the modern lyric.

OPPOSITE:

Rolling pasture at Cades Cove on a spring morning.
Great Smoky Mountains National Park, Tennessee/North Carolina

Lupine meadow adjoining a pond reflecting the Teton Range at dawn. *Grand Teton National Park, Wyoming*

*Earth fills her lap with pleasures
of her own.*

—WILLIAM WORDSWORTH

OPPOSITE:
Horsetail on a hillside above Pacific coast seastacks.
Ecola State Park, Oregon

Nature is heaven.

—EMILY DICKINSON

OPPOSITE:

Moss-covered tree trunks along Abrams Creek at Cades Cove.
Great Smoky Mountains National Park, Tennessee/North Carolina

ABOVE:

Cluster of false hellebore in early spring.
Shenandoah National Park, Virginia

ABOVE:

Three blossoms of Beavertail Cactus.
Death Valley National Monument, California

Manifest plainness,
Embrace simplicity,
Reduce selfishness,
Have few desires.

—LAO-TZU

Falls spilling over mossy rocks in the Roaring Fork Stream.
Great Smoky Mountains National Park, Tennessee/North Carolina

There is not room for Death.

—EMILY BRONTË

OPPOSITE:

Grove of red alder in the Soleduck River Valley.
Olympic National Park, Washington

*Faith is the substance of
things hoped for,
the evidence of
things not seen.*

—HEBREWS 11:10

OPPOSITE:
Behind the waterfalls in Horseshoe Canyon.
Starved Rock State Park, Illinois

*Eternity is not something that
begins after you are dead.
It is going on all the time.
We are in it now.*

—CHARLOTTE PERKINS GILMAN

Springtime at Galena Canyon, against the backdrop of
Death Valley and the Black Mountains.
Death Valley National Park, California

The Black River at Manitou Falls.
Pattison State Park, Wisconsin

Trunks of the coast redwoods in Cathedral Grove.
Muir Woods National Monument, California

Balsamroot blooms on the hillside of Christian Pond near Jackson Lake Lodge. *Grand Teton National Park, Wyoming*

ABOVE:

Lupine and valerian in bloom along a rock wall at Sunbeam Creek.
Mount Rainier National Park, Washington

OPPOSITE:

Cascading water on mossy rocks at Dark Hollow Falls in early spring.
Shenandoah National Park, Virginia

The sea possesses a power over one's moods that has the effect of a will. The sea can hypnotize.

—HENRIK IBSEN

OPPOSITE:

Surf and seastacks.
Bandon Beach, Oregon

Spring blossoms at the edge of the Big Sur headlands above the Pacific coast. *Monterey County, California*

*Deep in their roots
All flowers keep the light.*

—THEODORE ROETHKE

OPPOSITE:
Pink azalea and a view of the wooded ridges
of the Shenandoah River Valley.
Blue Ridge Parkway, Virginia

All flesh is grass, and all the goodliness thereof is as the flower of the field.

—Isaiah 40:6

OPPOSITE:

Hydrangea blossoms.
Washington Park Arboretum, Washington

Imagination is the eye of the soul.

—JOSEPH JOUBERT

OPPOSITE:

A thick, spreading canopy of live oak.
Savannah, Georgia

God Almighty first planted a
garden; and, indeed, it is the purest
of human pleasures.

—FRANCIS BACON

Flowering redbud in a spring hardwood forest.
Nelson Dewey State Park, Wisconsin

Lichen-covered rock
in a meadow of
wildflowers under the
Blacktail Deer Plateau.
*Yellowstone National Park,
Wyoming/Montana*

SUMMER

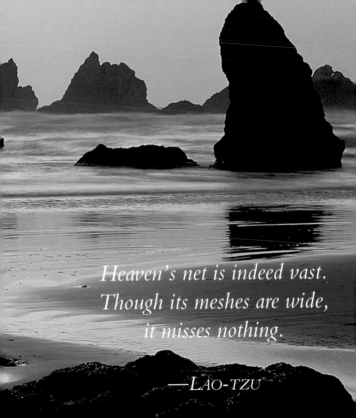

Heaven's net is indeed vast.
Though its meshes are wide,
it misses nothing.

—LAO-TZU

SUMMER

Where spring seems a succession of events, one blossoming, one set of birds appearing after the next, summer seems much more static, a single intensely experienced day that goes on like music repeating itself, day after day, week after week, even as it keeps growing thicker and taller, ever more voluminous.

In the forested landscape of eastern America the vegetation, leafing out, has cut off the sights, the distances and, instead of vistas, we feast on close-up images and sensations, smells that reawaken our earliest memories, tactile ones of transforming sunlight, of soothing water soaking into our skins. We see the mind not as a separate entity, but as part of a greater body. And the day seems divided into times when we are moving about, walking, riding, swimming, mowing a lawn, cramming life in through every pore, and other times when we are just sit-

PREVIOUS PAGE:
Sunset reflections at low tide with silhouetted seastacks.
Bandon Beach, Oregon

ting, enjoying a picnic under a shady tree, the sights of a yard, the momentary breeze, from a porch.

Everyone knows, listening in the dark, the dawn chorus of the birds, each successive moment louder than the last. For the next couple of hours everything is sharp, fresh, the woods astir with countless flittings high in the branches, the flower stalks waving back and forth, beautifully backlit by the still slanting, early morning sun. It is a great time to be out, up and about, and we each in our ways try to seize it, to accomplish what we can before the sun gets too vertical.

By mid-morning the woods are silent, making us all the more conscious in the heavy stillness of the mechanical calling crickets and cicadas, the murmuring of bees in a meadow, the whisk of a tail chasing a tormenting fly. It is a time of smells, too, the laundry-like freshness of newly mown grass, of the salt air at the seaside, the ripe, pungent odors of a barn. And we feel the grass, too, prickly against bare skin.

The hotter it is, the more we must don caps and wide-brimmed hats, and wear the looser trousers and

PREVIOUS PAGE:
Blue waters of Lake Crescent seen through big-leaf maple branches.
Olympic National Park, Washington

wide sleeves that will allow the air to irrigate our skins. For the same reasons we go out of our way to find shadows, taking refuge among the ferns of a forest, looking out from behind the curtain of a waterfall, watching a pair of painted butterflies playing over a pond.

By now it is time to seek out the cool relief of water, bathing, surfing, canoeing, sailing, or just lying in the sand soaking in the rays like a lizard on a wall. Little children, emancipated from their fenced yards, play unafraid at the edge of the waves. Others, slightly older, explore the tide-pools, or dive from a rock, remembering the different warmths of the water standing in a pond, the delicious mud at our feet, the tang of the salt long after we have emerged, teeth chattering, lips blue.

In the twilight the shadows become soft and alive again, the branches lift from the trees, more things of air than earth. Sitting out over a western fire, we feel ourselves surrounded in greens and blues, and in sounds, the hoarse croakings of a frog, the shrill peeping of another frog high in a tree, the differently pitched calls of a pack of coyotes, or the single, rare hoot of an owl. Just enough temptation in the mild air, under a now starlit sky, to pick up a flashlight, or better an infra-red lamp, and stroll forth once again.

ABOVE:
Brittlebush under a rock.
Anza-Borrego Desert State Park, California

OPPOSITE:
Still, blue waters of Lake Superior at Big Bay Point, Madeline Island.
Big Bay State Park, Wisconsin

Yaqui meadows and
flowering brittlebush
at the foot of Indian
Head Peak and the
San Ysidro Mountains.
*Anza-Borrego
Desert State Park,
California*

Energy is eternal delight.

—*WILLIAM BLAKE*

Those who lose dreaming are lost.

—*AUSTRALIAN ABORIGINAL
PROVERB*

OPPOSITE:

Two agave plants beneath the Chisos Mountains.
Big Bend National Park, Texas

*We are as near to heaven
by sea as by land!*

—SIR HUMPHREY GILBERT

OPPOSITE:
Tide pools expose the rocks at low tide.
Olympic National Park, Washington

Life begets life.
Energy creates energy.
It is by spending oneself
that one becomes rich.

—SARAH BERNHARDT

Pounding surf at Devil's Churn at Cape Perpetua.
Siuslaw National Forest, Oregon

*Joy is not in things;
it is in us.*

—RICHARD WAGNER

OPPOSITE:
The white water of Sunwapta Falls rushing over the rocks.
Jasper National Park, Alberta

All things change,
nothing perishes.

—OVID

Summer sun filtering down to the understory of a hardwood forest and
stream reflections in Ottawa Canyon.
Starved Rock State Park, Illinois

Beach naupaka covering
the volcanic cliffs above
Pailoa Bay.
*Waianapanapa State
Park, Hawaii*

BELOW:
Evening light highlighting driftwood and stones at Ruby Beach.
Olympic National Park, Washington

OPPOSITE:
Wildflower patterns in the Painted Hills.
John Day Fossil Beds National Monument, Oregon

The goal of life is living in agreement with nature.

—DIOGENES LAERTIUS

OPPOSITE:

Gathering clouds over West Tensleep Lake.
Bighorn National Forest, Wyoming

There is pleasure
in the pathless woods.

—LORD BYRON

Fragrant water lilies on the still water of the St. Croix River Flowage. *Near Gordon, Douglas County, Wisconsin*

ABOVE:

Pictured Rocks cliffs and Lake Superior surf from Miner's Beach.
Pictured Rocks National Lakeshore, Michigan

OPPOSITE:

Coastal cliffs at the mouth of Ohe'o Gulch.
Haleakala National Park, Hawaii

Morning light on the
Painted Hills.
*John Day Fossil Beds
National Monument,
Oregon*

All are but parts
of one stupendous whole,
Whose body nature is,
and God the soul.

—ALEXANDER POPE

OPPOSITE:
Mossy rocks and tidal pools at Oceanside Beach.
Tillamook County, Oregon

With the ancient is wisdom; and in length of days understanding.

—JOB 12:12

OPPOSITE:

Hoodoos on the slickrock sandstone under the White Cliffs.
Zion National Park, Utah

Sunset and silhouetted
peaks from
Queen Canyon.
*KOFA National Wildlife
Refuge, Arizona*

FALL

There is a harmony in autumn,
and a lustre in its sky.

—PERCY BYSSHE SHELLEY

FALL

"Season of mists and mellow fruitfulness," wrote Keats, thinking of the British autumn. Ours is somewhat sharper, shorter. The first snows can arrive very early, by mid-October out on the prairies, by early November in New England. And unlike the British monochrome, however splashed with touches of yellow, ours boasts a range of color unlike anywhere else, a revolving kaleidoscope as we stare up at it of reds, pinks, oranges, golds, set off in turn by the dark piercing blues of pond and sky.

Except in the monsoonal southwest, where the September rains have launched a reflowering of the pink earth, blooms are comparatively rare. But that makes the blue of a last mountain gentian, the uncluttered opulence of a reblooming rose, a monkshood and an aster in the

PREVIOUS PAGE:
Roche Ronde under afternoon clouds, reflected in
wetland along the Athabasca River.
Jasper National Park, Alberta

forest, all the more poignant. And the dearth of flowers is almost overlooked, such is the splendor of the tall pluming grasses, risen at the edge of a pond, the gustatory thrill that we find hunting chanterelle mushrooms on a forest slope, stooping from one burst of yellow to the next.

In the West, fall belongs to the stands of slender, golden-yellow aspen. In New England the preeminent tree is the giant sugar maple. The dryer the fall, and the sharper the first frost, the more glorious the spectrum that it gives. In a hardwood forest everything else pitches in, from the first sycamores to the last willows and oaks, turning and then slowly drifting down. The peak time where I live is the mid-October, Columbus Day weekend, the leaf-viewers in their tweeds almost as colorful as the leaves themselves. Then, to the dismay of everyone but the children tumbling in the piles, the leaves are covering everything and turning brown.

The fall has a curve to it as the sharpening frosts blanket the new distances with morning mist. In the midst, however, of this progression there is always that ten days of disbelief we call "Indian summer." We know we are being fooled, but that does not keep us from wanting to be out in it, hanging on a ladder, immersed in the reds and greens of an apple tree, riding a horse at the edge of a

plowed field, or playing a game of soccer or touch football. Up above, in the clearest of skies, we can hear the honking of the flying wedges of migrating geese, and we spot from the top of a hill the revolving kettles of the hawks.

Then it's over, and we are commemorating what we have lost with the wreaths of dried flowers and Indian corn that we set by our doorways, and all those rows of ghoulishly exuberant pumpkins. And the pumpkins remind us in turn of the anarchic bang with which the autumn goes out at Halloween.

With the distances that now are starting to open, privacy recedes and fall brings a return of social awareness. We notice the smoke of a neighbor's fire, a hunter's shot crackling out from the forest. In cities it is the time when everything comes back to life after the desertion of the summer. Clothes look new, plays and art shows open, and all the books of the year seem to be published at once. In summer, we are nature's slaves. In fall, we become human beings again, people who have hands, who make things.

OPPOSITE:

Ferns and moss-covered logs.
Olympic National Park, Washington

ABOVE:

Mussels and seaweed at low tide on Deer Isle.
Hancock County, Maine

OPPOSITE:

Sunrise on the rocky coast near Newport Cove
and Otter Cliffs in the distance.
Acadia National Park, Maine

The course of Nature
is the art of God.

—EDWARD YOUNG

OPPOSITE:
Fall colors on beech and rhododendron branches
over stream in Cades Cove.
Great Smoky Mountains National Park, Tennessee/North Carolina

ABOVE:

Fall-colored western larch on a granite wall.
Alpine Lakes Wilderness Area, Washington

OPPOSITE:

Prusik Peak above Viviane Lake.
Alpine Lakes Wilderness Area, Washington

Peace is liberty in tranquility.

—*CICERO*

Moss-covered trees and wood sorrel ground cover on the Maple Glade Rainforest Trail. *Olympic National Park, Washington*

*The world is the sum-total
of all our possibilities.*

—JOSÉ ORTEGA Y GASSET

OPPOSITE:
Carp River winding through the fall-colored hardwood forest.
Porcupine Mountains Wilderness State Park, Michigan

The Unbearable Lightness of Being.

—MILAN KUNDERA

OPPOSITE:

Presque Isle River flowing over ledges and falls bordered by fall foliage.
Porcupine Mountains Wilderness State Park, Michigan

East Flat Top Mountain
above the stony banks of
the Saint Mary River.
*Glacier National Park,
Montana*

We have been the recipients of the choicest bounties of heaven.

—ABRAHAM LINCOLN

East Flat Top Mountain rising above the golden grasses of Two Dog Flats.
Glacier National Park, Montana

Sugar maples and
yellow birch forest
above Duck Brook.
*Acadia National Park,
Maine*

The Grand Canyon under approaching storm clouds as seen from Hopi Point. *Grand Canyon National Park, Arizona*

And the leaves of the tree were for the healing of the nations.

—REVELATION OF ST. JOHN 22:2

OPPOSITE:
Fall hardwood forest on the west rim of Illinois Canyon.
Starved Rock State Park, Illinois

*As long
as we perform our works
in order to get to heaven
we are simply
on the wrong track.*

—MEISTER ECKHART

OPPOSITE:
Morning sun on the cliff face of Palisade Head
and Lake Superior in early fall.
Palisade Head State Park, Minnesota

Lake of the Clouds in the
Carp River Valley
bordered by brilliant
fall foliage.
*Porcupine Mountains
Wilderness State Park,
Michigan*

*If you have not exhausted the scope
of seeing and hearing,
How can you realize the wideness
of the world?*

—PO CHÜ-I

OPPOSITE:
Red Alder trunk with Vine Maple cloaked in fall colors.
Mount Baker-Snoqualmie National Forest, Washington

ABOVE:

Wahkeena Creek tumbling through fall forest.
Columbia Gorge National Scenic Area, Oregon

OPPOSITE:

Fall-colored forest canopy.
Matthiessen State Park, Illinois

Unexpectedly you find it,
welling upwards in the empty tree.

—RAINER MARIA RILKE

Weathered trunks against the fall colors of a hardwood forest.
Hiawatha National Forest, Michigan

Hoodoos and pinnacles
in Agua Canyon.
*Bryce National Park,
Utah*

WINTER

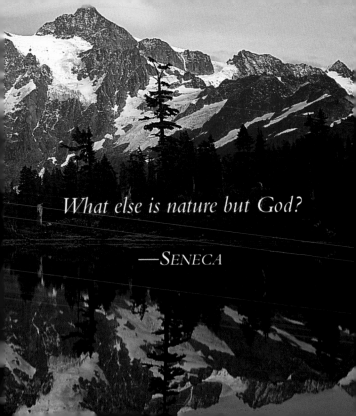

What else is nature but God?

—SENECA

WINTER

In winter our eyes, the most rational of our senses, come into their own. Even indoors, we find ourselves constantly being summoned to a window: on the east side of the house a dawn more unearthly than any yet, yellows, tender blues, pinks; or up in the mountains, against the dark of a shadowed snow-covered valley, a series of peaks being touched, one by one, into bluest day; then, in late afternoon, a livid sunset, brief, but far more memorable than those of any other time.

Walking about, we train our eyes like hawks, reveling in the sudden clarity of a home landscape that seems newly revealed. Far away fields come into focus, while shadows add a dimension of mystery, of welcome color, to the sharp contrasts of snow fields and forest, black and white. And the white itself, of a waterfall, of a cliff's drip-

PREVIOUS PAGE:
Reflection of moonrise and Mount Shukan in Picture Lake.
Mt. Baker-Snoqualmie National Forest, Washington

ping icicles, seems not white, but an otherworldly pale cerulean blue or jade green.

Snow itself, as any child knows, is a prism of color refracting the changes in the light. Just stand in a field and cross your eyes until the prisms start to sparkle and glow, making a virtual rainbow in which you are surrounded. Light is life and in winter, perhaps because there is not quite enough, it seems all the more precious for the color with which it bathes all that we are taking in, and for the constant transformations in what we are seeing that it creates.

This visual heightening makes the odd sound, carried from afar in the thin air, all the more eerie. Call to mind the ghostly cracking of a forest limb, the image of loneliness created by an unseen oar striking the water, the mysterious, not to say ominous, cracks and rumblings going on beneath the lake ice we are skating on, the sensuous whistling of a pair of cross-country skis gliding along a trail, the scrape of a shovel clearing a path, of an ax chopping wood, hour after hour, one afternoon after the next, for a cabin's warmth.

If we are our eyes, birds are the eyes of the landscape. When the last leaves disappear, there are still the omnivorous crows, black spots on a tree. Wherever there are

berries, there may be a flock of sweetly piping cedar waxwings, crested heads, warm tans and golds looking gloriously drunken against the snow. And sometimes, for a few days, every couple of years, there may appear at our feeders a flock of evening grosbeaks, their color the gold of a winter afternoon. Like the winter itself, these visitors startle us with their mysteriousness, their subtle beauty.

OPPOSITE:
Gold aspen groves on a hillside below the San Juan mountain peaks.
Uncompahgre National Forest, Colorado

There is a pleasure
in the pathless woods,
There is a rapture
on the lonely shore,
There is society,
where none intrudes,
By the deep sea,
and music in its roar.

—LORD BYRON

OPPOSITE:
Sunset over broken ice floes in Grand Traverse Bay, Lake Michigan.
Grand Traverse County, Michigan

*The silence of the gods
is the silence of the earth.*

—KRISHNAMURTI

OPPOSITE:

Santa Elena Canyon and Mesa de Aguila reflected in the Rio Grande.
Big Bend National Park, Texas

ABOVE:

Ice-encircled rocks in the North Fork Nooksack River.
Mount Baker-Snoqualmie National Forest, Washington

OPPOSITE:

Paradise Park's lush green ridges sweeping toward Mount Rainier.
Mount Rainier National Park, Washington

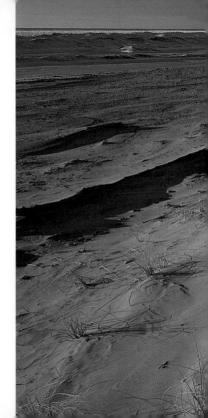

Late afternoon sun on the dunes, grasses, and frozen shoreline of Lake Michigan. *Muskegon State Park, Michigan*

Mountains are the scribblings of time on the surface of the land.

—HARRY MIDDLETON

OPPOSITE:

Early winter storm clearing over West Elk Mountain
with reflections in Lost Lake Slough.
Gunnison National Forest, Colorado

Fight the good fight of faith,
lay hold on eternal life.

—1 TIMOTHY 6:12

Silver light of dusk playing on the tide pools and seastacks of Ruby Beach. *Olympic National Park, Washington*

Silence is deep as Eternity.
Speech is shallow as Time.

—THOMAS CARLYLE

Telescope Peak and eroded hills drenched in
morning light, seen from Zabriskie Point.
Death Valley National Park, California

Deep red sandstone of
Fire Canyon surmounted
by rising moon.
*Valley of Fire State Park,
Nevada*

*The clearest way into the universe
is through a forest wilderness.*

—JOHN MUIR

OPPOSITE:
Snow-covered banks along the Wenatchee River.
Wenatchee National Forest, Washington

Nothing is permanent but change.

—HERACLITUS

OPPOSITE:

Winter sun shining on the San Juan peaks
and on the snow banks of Canyon Creek.
Uncompahgre National Forest, Colorado

Come forth into the light of things,
Let Nature be your teacher.

—WILLIAM WORDSWORTH

OPPOSITE:
Morning sun on frosted branches along the snow-covered
banks of the North Fork Nooksack River.
Mount Baker-Snoqualmie National Forest, Washington

BELOW:

Snow and ice-covered banks in the Snoqualmie River.
Mount Baker-Snoqualmie National Forest, Washington

OPPOSITE:

Steam venting from Castle Geyser on a winter morning.
Yellowstone National Park, Wyoming/Montana

The universe is change;
our life is what our thoughts
make it.

—MARCUS AURELIUS ANTONINUS

OPPOSITE:
Contoured rain patterns in snow near Austin Pass.
Mount Baker-Snoqualmie National Forest, Washington

Hoar-frosted branches
on winter pines.
*LaSalle County,
Illinois*

Winter profile of
Grand Teton and
surrounding peaks.
*Grand Teton
National Park,
Wyoming*

*Just trust yourself, then you will
know how to live.*

—JOHANN WOLFGANG
VON GOETHE

OPPOSITE:
Rime ice on trees and snow cover in the Upper Geyser Basin.
Yellowstone National Park, Wyoming/Montana

*Cultivate peace and harmony
with all.*

—GEORGE WASHINGTON

Morning light on the
glaciers of Mount Rainier,
reflected onto the
icy waters of
Upper Tipsoo Lake.
*Mount Rainier
National Park,
Washington*

INDEX

PROJECT EDITOR: Raegan Randolph
DESIGNER: Paula Winicur
PRODUCTION MANAGER: Louise Kurtz

First edition
10 9 8 7 6 5 4 3 2 1

Library of Congress Cataloging-in-Publication Data
Donnelly, Terry.
Heaven on earth/photographs by Terry Donnelly; text by Robin
Magowan—1st ed.
p.   cm. — (A miniSeries book)
ISBN 0-7892-0588-2
1. Nature Pictorial works. I. Magowan, Robin. II. Title. III. Series.
QH81.D67 1999
508'.022'2—dc21   99-33904
CIP

FRONT COVER: Moonrise over Bow Lake and Bow Peak. *Banff National Park, Alberta*
BACK COVER: Green alternating ridges of Wailena Gulch. *Near Hakuhee Point, Maui, Hawaii*
SPINE: The fiery drama of a single cultivated flower.

About the Photographer

Terry Donnelly is an accomplished nature photographer whose specialty is sweeping and intimate views of the American landscape in all seasons. He has contributed his work to a number of books, magazines, and calendars, including Abbeville's *Heaven on Earth* engagement and wall calendars. He lives in Washington.

About the Author

Robin Magowan has written eleven books, including Abbeville's *America, America* and *Fabled Cities of Central Asia*, his autobiography, *Memoirs of a Minotaur*, and seven volumes of poetry. He lives in rural Connecticut.

Also Available in this Series

- *Barbie: Four Decades of Fashion* 0-7892-0552-1 • 192 pages • $5.95
- *Cats up Close* 0-7892-0510-6 • 192 pages • $5.95
- *Elvis: His Life in Pictures* 0-7892-0509-2 • 192 pages • $5.95
- *Horses* 0-7892-0526-2 • 192 pages • $5.95
- *Tropical Cocktails* 0-7892-0554-8 • 192 pages • $5.95
- *Weddings* 0-7892-0524-6 • 192 page • $5.95